100 Interview Questions to Ace that interview!

For Business Analysts

Jason Zyger

Are you a Business Analyst preparing for an interview?

These 100 questions curated from multiple firms and successful Business Analysts, will guarantee you get that job!

This Book is one of the biggest Investments you can make in your career.

1. **Can you describe your understanding of the role of a business analyst within an organization?**
   - "As a business analyst, my primary role is to act as a liaison between business stakeholders and technical teams. I facilitate communication and collaboration to ensure that projects align with the organization's goals and objectives. This involves gathering and analysing requirements, identifying opportunities for process improvement, and translating business needs into actionable solutions. Ultimately, my goal is to drive positive change and help the organization achieve its strategic vision."
2. **What methodologies or frameworks do you prefer to use when conducting business analysis, and why?**
   - "I prefer to use a combination of Agile and Lean methodologies for their emphasis on collaboration, flexibility, and continuous improvement. Agile allows for iterative development and quick adaptation to changing requirements, while Lean focuses on eliminating waste and maximizing efficiency. By incorporating elements of both approaches, I can deliver value to stakeholders more effectively and respond quickly to evolving business needs."
3. **How do you approach gathering and analyzing requirements from stakeholders?**
   - "I start by conducting stakeholder interviews and workshops to understand their needs, goals, and expectations. I use techniques like brainstorming sessions, focus groups, and surveys to gather input from a diverse range of perspectives. Once requirements are gathered, I prioritize them based on business value and feasibility, and then analyze them to identify dependencies, conflicts, and potential risks."
4. **Can you provide an example of a challenging project you worked on as a business analyst and how you overcame obstacles?**
   - "In a previous project, we were tasked with implementing a new CRM system across multiple departments within the organization. One of the main challenges we faced was resistance from key stakeholders who were hesitant to adopt

new technology. To overcome this obstacle, I organized demos and training sessions to address their concerns and showcase the benefits of the new system. I also worked closely with project sponsors to secure their support and address any issues or roadblocks that arose."

5. **How do you ensure that your analysis aligns with the overall business objectives and strategy?**
    - "I always start by consulting with business leaders and key stakeholders to understand the organization's strategic goals and priorities. I then use this information to guide my analysis and ensure that all recommendations are aligned with the overarching business strategy. Throughout the project lifecycle, I regularly communicate with stakeholders to validate assumptions, gather feedback, and make adjustments as needed to stay on track."

6. **What techniques do you use to identify opportunities for process improvement or optimization?**
    - "I use a variety of techniques to identify opportunities for process improvement, including process mapping, root cause analysis, and benchmarking against industry best practices. I also leverage data analysis to pinpoint inefficiencies and bottlenecks in existing processes. By identifying areas for improvement, I can develop targeted solutions that streamline operations, reduce costs, and enhance overall efficiency."

7. **How do you handle conflicting priorities or requirements from different stakeholders?**
    - "I approach conflicting priorities by facilitating open dialogue and collaboration among stakeholders to find common ground. This may involve conducting stakeholder workshops or meetings to clarify expectations, resolve conflicts, and prioritize requirements based on their impact on business objectives. If necessary, I escalate conflicts to project sponsors or senior leadership for resolution, while ensuring transparency and accountability throughout the process."

8. **Can you discuss your experience with data analysis and how you utilize data to inform business decisions?**

- "I have extensive experience with data analysis tools and techniques, including data visualization, statistical analysis, and predictive modeling. I use these tools to analyze large datasets and identify trends, patterns, and insights that can inform strategic decision-making. By leveraging data-driven insights, I can help organizations make informed decisions, identify new opportunities, and mitigate risks."

9. **How do you ensure effective communication between technical and non-technical stakeholders during the project lifecycle?**
    - "I use a variety of communication strategies to ensure effective collaboration between technical and non-technical stakeholders. This may include using plain language to explain technical concepts, visual aids such as diagrams or prototypes to illustrate ideas, and regular status updates or progress reports to keep all stakeholders informed and engaged. I also encourage feedback and questions to ensure that everyone has a clear understanding of project objectives and requirements."

10. **Can you walk us through your approach to creating business requirement documents and other project artifacts?**
    - "I start by conducting thorough stakeholder interviews and workshops to gather requirements, using techniques such as user stories, use cases, or process flows to document findings. I then organize these requirements into clear and concise business requirement documents (BRDs) or other project artifacts, ensuring that they are comprehensive, well-defined, and aligned with stakeholder expectations. Throughout the process, I collaborate closely with stakeholders to validate requirements and incorporate feedback, making adjustments as needed to ensure accuracy and completeness."

11. **How do you stay updated on industry trends and best practices in business analysis?**
    - "I stay updated on industry trends and best practices through a variety of channels, including attending industry

conferences, webinars, and workshops. I also regularly read industry publications, blogs, and research reports to stay informed about emerging trends and innovations in business analysis. Additionally, I participate in online forums and communities to share knowledge, exchange ideas, and learn from other professionals in the field."

12. **Can you provide an example of a successful project where your analysis led to tangible business outcomes?**
    - "In a recent project, I conducted a thorough analysis of customer feedback and market research to identify opportunities for product improvement. Based on my analysis, I recommended several strategic changes to the product design and features. As a result, customer satisfaction increased by 20%, and sales revenue grew by 15% within six months of implementing the changes. This project demonstrated the tangible impact of effective analysis on driving business success and customer satisfaction."

13. **How do you handle situations where the scope of a project changes mid-stream?**
    - "When the scope of a project changes mid-stream, I first assess the impact of the changes on project objectives, timelines, and resources. I then communicate with stakeholders to understand the reasons for the change and evaluate potential alternatives or solutions. If necessary, I update project documentation, such as the project plan or requirements documents, to reflect the new scope. Throughout the process, I prioritize transparency, collaboration, and flexibility to ensure that the project remains on track and delivers value to stakeholders."

14. **Can you discuss your experience with conducting user acceptance testing (UAT) and ensuring that deliverables meet user expectations?**
    - "I have extensive experience with conducting user acceptance testing (UAT) to ensure that deliverables meet user expectations and business requirements. I collaborate closely with end users to define acceptance criteria and

develop test plans that align with their needs and objectives. During the testing phase, I coordinate test activities, track defects, and facilitate communication between the project team and stakeholders. I also provide training and support to end users to ensure a smooth transition to the new system or solution."

15. **How do you prioritize tasks and manage your time effectively as a business analyst?**
    - "I prioritize tasks and manage my time effectively by using tools such as task lists, calendars, and project management software. I start by identifying critical tasks and deadlines and then allocate time and resources accordingly. I also use techniques such as the Eisenhower Matrix to prioritize tasks based on urgency and importance. Additionally, I regularly review and adjust my priorities as needed to ensure that I stay focused on high-value activities and deliverables."

16. **Can you describe a situation where you had to facilitate a difficult conversation or resolve a conflict between stakeholders?**
    - "In a previous project, there was a disagreement between two key stakeholders regarding the prioritization of project requirements. To resolve the conflict, I facilitated a series of meetings to clarify each stakeholder's concerns, objectives, and priorities. I used active listening and conflict resolution techniques to foster open communication and mutual understanding. Through constructive dialogue and compromise, we were able to reach a consensus and move forward with a shared vision for the project."

17. **How do you ensure that your recommendations are feasible and actionable for the organization?**
    - "I ensure that my recommendations are feasible and actionable by conducting thorough analysis, considering factors such as resource availability, technical constraints, and organizational capabilities. I also collaborate with subject matter experts and key stakeholders to validate assumptions and identify potential risks or challenges. Additionally, I prioritize recommendations based on their potential impact,

feasibility, and alignment with the organization's goals and objectives."

18. **Can you discuss a time when you had to influence stakeholders or project team members to adopt a new approach or solution?**
    - "In a recent project, I proposed a new approach to streamline a complex business process and improve efficiency. However, there was initial resistance from some stakeholders who were hesitant to change existing workflows. To overcome this resistance, I developed a compelling business case that highlighted the benefits of the proposed approach, such as cost savings, time efficiency, and improved customer satisfaction. I also engaged with key stakeholders individually to address their concerns and gain their support. Through effective communication and stakeholder engagement, I was able to successfully implement the new approach and achieve the desired outcomes."

19. **How do you handle feedback, both positive and constructive, on your analysis and recommendations?**
    - "I welcome feedback as an opportunity for growth and improvement. When receiving positive feedback, I express gratitude and use it to reinforce successful practices and behaviors. When receiving constructive feedback, I approach it with an open mind and view it as an opportunity to learn and grow. I reflect on the feedback, identify areas for improvement, and take proactive steps to address any gaps or weaknesses in my analysis or recommendations. I also seek feedback from colleagues, mentors, and stakeholders to ensure continuous improvement and development."

20. **Finally, why do you believe you are the best fit for this business analyst position?**
    - "I believe I am the best fit for this business analyst position because of my diverse experience, strong analytical skills, and passion for driving positive change within organizations. I have a proven track record of delivering value to stakeholders through effective analysis, strategic planning, and collaboration. I am also committed to ongoing learning

and professional development, which enables me to stay current with industry trends and best practices. I am excited about the opportunity to contribute my skills and expertise to your team and help achieve your business goals."

21. **Can you describe a time when you had to work on multiple projects simultaneously? How did you prioritize tasks and manage your time effectively?**
    - "In a previous role, I often had to juggle multiple projects with competing deadlines. To prioritize tasks, I used a combination of time management techniques, such as setting clear goals, breaking tasks into smaller, manageable chunks, and using tools like Gantt charts or Kanban boards to track progress. I also communicated regularly with project stakeholders to manage expectations and ensure alignment with project objectives."

22. **How do you approach conducting stakeholder analysis and identifying key stakeholders for a project?**
    - "When conducting stakeholder analysis, I start by identifying all potential stakeholders and mapping out their roles, interests, and influence levels. I then prioritize stakeholders based on their level of impact on the project and their level of support or resistance. This helps me determine the most effective strategies for engaging with stakeholders and managing their expectations throughout the project lifecycle."

23. **Can you discuss your experience with facilitating requirements gathering sessions and eliciting requirements from stakeholders?**
    - "I have extensive experience with facilitating requirements gathering sessions and eliciting requirements from stakeholders using techniques such as brainstorming, interviews, surveys, and workshops. I create a collaborative environment that encourages open communication and active participation from all stakeholders. I also use visualization tools such as whiteboards or sticky notes to

capture and organize requirements in real-time, ensuring that everyone's input is captured and documented accurately."

24. **How do you ensure that project documentation, such as business requirement documents (BRDs) and functional specifications, is clear, concise, and comprehensive?**
    - "I ensure that project documentation is clear, concise, and comprehensive by following established standards and best practices for documentation. This includes using standardized templates, organizing information logically, and using clear and unambiguous language. I also collaborate closely with stakeholders to review and validate documentation, incorporating feedback and making revisions as needed to ensure accuracy and completeness."

25. **Can you provide an example of a time when you had to adapt to changes in project scope or requirements? How did you handle the situation?**
    - "In a recent project, there was a significant change in project scope due to shifting business priorities. To adapt to the changes, I conducted a thorough impact assessment to understand the implications on project objectives, timelines, and resources. I then communicated with stakeholders to discuss alternative approaches and develop a revised project plan that aligned with the new scope. Throughout the process, I prioritized transparency and collaboration to ensure that all stakeholders were informed and involved in decision-making."

26. **How do you handle situations where stakeholders have conflicting or competing priorities?**
    - "When stakeholders have conflicting priorities, I facilitate open communication and collaboration to understand their underlying interests and concerns. I use techniques such as negotiation, consensus-building, and compromise to find common ground and reach mutually acceptable solutions. If necessary, I escalate conflicts to project sponsors or senior leadership for resolution, while ensuring transparency and accountability throughout the process."

27. **Can you discuss your experience with creating and managing project budgets as a business analyst?**
    - "I have experience creating and managing project budgets by collaborating with project sponsors, finance teams, and other stakeholders to define budgetary constraints and allocations. I work closely with project managers to develop cost estimates, track expenses, and monitor budget variances throughout the project lifecycle. I also identify opportunities for cost savings or optimization and make recommendations to stakeholders to ensure that projects are delivered within budgetary constraints."
28. **How do you ensure that deliverables meet quality standards and are aligned with stakeholder expectations?**
    - "I ensure that deliverables meet quality standards and stakeholder expectations by conducting thorough quality assurance activities, such as reviews, inspections, and testing. I work closely with stakeholders to define acceptance criteria and develop test plans that align with their needs and objectives. I also provide training and support to end users to ensure a smooth transition to the new system or solution."
29. **Can you discuss your experience with risk management and how you identify, assess, and mitigate risks on projects?**
    - "I have experience with risk management by identifying, assessing, and mitigating risks on projects. I conduct risk assessments to identify potential threats or opportunities that may impact project objectives, timelines, or resources. I then develop risk mitigation strategies to minimize the likelihood and impact of risks, such as contingency plans, risk transfer, or risk avoidance strategies. Throughout the project lifecycle, I regularly monitor risks and take proactive steps to address emerging threats or capitalize on opportunities."
30. **How do you ensure effective communication and collaboration within project teams, especially in virtual or remote work environments?**
    - "I ensure effective communication and collaboration within project teams by leveraging technology tools such as video conferencing, project management software, and

collaboration platforms. I establish clear communication channels, expectations, and protocols to facilitate regular updates, progress reports, and feedback loops. I also foster a culture of transparency, trust, and accountability, where team members feel comfortable sharing ideas, asking questions, and addressing concerns. Additionally, I schedule regular team meetings and check-ins to maintain engagement and alignment, especially in virtual or remote work environments."

31. **How do you approach conducting gap analysis to identify discrepancies between current and desired states in a project?**
    - "I approach conducting gap analysis by first defining the current state and desired future state of the project. I then identify the gaps or discrepancies between the two states by comparing factors such as processes, systems, resources, and performance metrics. This helps me understand where improvements or changes are needed to bridge the gap and achieve the desired outcomes. I collaborate closely with stakeholders to prioritize gap closure activities and develop actionable plans to address identified gaps."

32. **Can you discuss your experience with creating and maintaining project schedules or timelines?**
    - "I have experience creating and maintaining project schedules or timelines by developing detailed project plans that outline key tasks, milestones, and dependencies. I use project management software such as Microsoft Project or Trello to create Gantt charts or Kanban boards that visualize project timelines and progress. I also regularly monitor and update project schedules to track progress, identify potential delays or risks, and adjust timelines as needed to ensure project objectives are met."

33. **How do you ensure that project requirements are effectively communicated to technical teams for implementation?**

- "I ensure that project requirements are effectively communicated to technical teams for implementation by developing clear and concise documentation, such as functional specifications or user stories, that outline the requirements in detail. I also conduct regular meetings or workshops with technical teams to review requirements, clarify any ambiguities, and address questions or concerns. Additionally, I provide ongoing support and clarification throughout the development process to ensure that requirements are understood and implemented accurately."

34. **Can you provide an example of a time when you had to manage stakeholder expectations on a project?**
    - "In a previous project, there was a discrepancy between stakeholder expectations and project scope due to changing business priorities. To manage stakeholder expectations, I conducted regular communication and updates to keep stakeholders informed of project progress, challenges, and changes. I also facilitated discussions to set realistic expectations and negotiate trade-offs between scope, schedule, and resources. By maintaining open communication and transparency, I was able to build trust and confidence with stakeholders and successfully manage their expectations throughout the project."

35. **How do you approach conducting feasibility studies to assess the viability of proposed projects or solutions?**
    - "I approach conducting feasibility studies by first defining the objectives and scope of the proposed project or solution. I then gather relevant data and information, such as market research, cost estimates, risk assessments, and technical requirements, to evaluate its feasibility. I analyze the data to identify potential benefits, risks, and constraints and assess whether the project aligns with organizational goals and resources. Based on the findings, I make recommendations to stakeholders on the feasibility and viability of the proposed project or solution."

36. **Can you discuss your experience with conducting business process modeling and optimization?**

- "I have experience conducting business process modeling and optimization by analyzing existing processes, identifying inefficiencies or bottlenecks, and designing improved or optimized processes. I use techniques such as process mapping, swimlane diagrams, and value stream mapping to visualize and analyze workflows. I also collaborate with stakeholders to identify opportunities for automation, standardization, or streamlining to improve efficiency, reduce costs, and enhance overall performance."

37. **How do you ensure that project deliverables are aligned with regulatory or compliance requirements?**
    - "I ensure that project deliverables are aligned with regulatory or compliance requirements by conducting thorough research and analysis to understand relevant laws, regulations, and industry standards. I work closely with legal and compliance teams to identify applicable requirements and ensure that project plans, requirements, and deliverables are designed to meet or exceed regulatory standards. I also conduct regular reviews and audits to verify compliance throughout the project lifecycle."

38. **Can you provide an example of a time when you had to lead a cross-functional team on a project?**
    - "In a previous project, I led a cross-functional team comprised of members from different departments, including IT, operations, and finance, to implement a new enterprise resource planning (ERP) system. I facilitated regular meetings and workshops to align team members on project objectives, roles, and responsibilities. I also established clear communication channels and protocols to facilitate collaboration and decision-making. Through effective leadership and teamwork, we successfully implemented the ERP system on time and within budget."

39. **How do you approach conducting post-project reviews or lessons learned sessions to identify areas for improvement?**
    - "I approach conducting post-project reviews or lessons learned sessions by gathering feedback from project stakeholders, including team members, sponsors, and

customers, through surveys, interviews, or focus groups. I analyze the feedback to identify areas of success, challenges, and opportunities for improvement. I then facilitate discussions to discuss lessons learned, identify best practices, and develop actionable recommendations for future projects. By promoting a culture of continuous improvement, we can leverage insights from past experiences to drive better outcomes in future projects."

40. **Can you discuss your long-term career goals and how this position aligns with them?**
    - "My long-term career goal is to continue growing and developing as a business analyst, expanding my expertise and leadership skills to drive positive change and innovation within organizations. I see this position as an opportunity to contribute my skills and experience to a dynamic team, tackle new challenges, and make a meaningful impact on business outcomes. I am excited about the opportunity to grow professionally and personally and to contribute to the success of the organization."

41. **How do you approach identifying and managing project dependencies and interdependencies?**
    - "I approach identifying and managing project dependencies by conducting thorough analysis and mapping out relationships between tasks, activities, and resources. I use techniques such as network diagrams or dependency matrices to visualize dependencies and understand their impact on project timelines and objectives. I also establish clear communication channels and protocols to coordinate dependencies and address any issues or conflicts that arise."

42. **Can you discuss your experience with conducting stakeholder impact analysis to assess the potential effects of a project on various stakeholders?**
    - "I have experience conducting stakeholder impact analysis by identifying and assessing the needs, interests, and concerns of different stakeholders affected by a project. I use techniques such as stakeholder mapping or power/interest

grids to categorize stakeholders based on their level of influence and impact. I then analyze the potential effects of the project on each stakeholder group and develop strategies to mitigate risks, address concerns, and maximize positive outcomes for all stakeholders."

43. **How do you ensure that project communication plans are effective in keeping stakeholders informed and engaged throughout the project lifecycle?**
    - "I ensure that project communication plans are effective by developing clear communication objectives, channels, and protocols that align with project goals and stakeholder needs. I establish regular communication schedules and formats, such as status updates, meetings, or newsletters, to keep stakeholders informed of project progress, milestones, and key decisions. I also encourage two-way communication and feedback to foster engagement and collaboration among stakeholders."

44. **Can you provide an example of a time when you had to manage project risks effectively to prevent or mitigate potential issues?**
    - "In a previous project, we encountered unexpected delays due to a vendor's failure to deliver critical components on time. To manage this risk effectively, I developed a contingency plan that included alternative suppliers and expedited shipping options. I also communicated with stakeholders proactively to keep them informed of the situation and the steps being taken to mitigate the impact. By implementing the contingency plan promptly, we were able to minimize delays and keep the project on track."

45. **How do you approach conducting root cause analysis to identify underlying factors contributing to project issues or challenges?**
    - "I approach conducting root cause analysis by asking 'why' multiple times to uncover deeper layers of causation behind project issues or challenges. I use techniques such as fishbone diagrams, 5 Whys, or Ishikawa diagrams to visualize and analyze the relationships between different factors and

identify the root causes of problems. I then develop targeted solutions or corrective actions to address the root causes and prevent similar issues from recurring in the future."

46. **Can you discuss your experience with facilitating workshops or focus groups to gather input and feedback from stakeholders?**
    - "I have experience facilitating workshops or focus groups to gather input and feedback from stakeholders using structured facilitation techniques and activities. I design workshop agendas and exercises that encourage active participation, creativity, and collaboration among participants. I also use facilitation tools such as brainstorming, affinity diagramming, or SWOT analysis to generate ideas, prioritize options, and make decisions collaboratively. By creating a supportive and inclusive environment, I can effectively elicit valuable insights and perspectives from stakeholders."

47. **How do you ensure that project deliverables meet accessibility standards and accommodate diverse user needs?**
    - "I ensure that project deliverables meet accessibility standards and accommodate diverse user needs by incorporating accessibility considerations into the design and development process from the outset. I collaborate with accessibility experts, user experience designers, and subject matter experts to identify accessibility requirements and best practices. I also conduct usability testing with diverse user groups, including individuals with disabilities, to identify barriers and make necessary adjustments to ensure that project deliverables are inclusive and accessible to all users."

48. **Can you provide an example of a time when you had to manage conflicting priorities or demands from project stakeholders?**
    - "In a previous project, we faced conflicting priorities between different stakeholder groups regarding the allocation of project resources. To manage this situation effectively, I facilitated discussions to understand the underlying interests and concerns of each stakeholder group. I then worked

collaboratively with stakeholders to negotiate trade-offs, prioritize requirements, and develop a consensus-driven approach that balanced competing demands while maximizing overall project value. By fostering open communication and collaboration, we were able to reach mutually acceptable solutions that satisfied all stakeholders."

49. **How do you approach conducting user training and change management activities to support the adoption of new systems or processes?**
    - "I approach conducting user training and change management activities by developing tailored training plans and materials that address the specific needs and preferences of end users. I use a combination of training methods, such as in-person workshops, online tutorials, and job aids, to accommodate different learning styles and preferences. I also incorporate change management principles and techniques, such as communication plans, stakeholder engagement, and readiness assessments, to prepare users for the transition and minimize resistance to change. By providing comprehensive training and support, I can ensure a smooth and successful adoption of new systems or processes."

50. **Finally, how do you stay motivated and resilient in the face of challenges or setbacks in your work as a business analyst?**
    - "I stay motivated and resilient in the face of challenges or setbacks by maintaining a positive mindset, focusing on solutions rather than problems, and seeking support from colleagues, mentors, and professional networks. I also practice self-care and stress management techniques, such as exercise, mindfulness, and time management, to maintain balance and perspective. Additionally, I view challenges as opportunities for growth and learning, and I use each experience as a chance to improve my skills, expand my knowledge, and become a better business analyst."

51. **How do you prioritize requirements when faced with conflicting stakeholder demands?**

- "When prioritizing requirements, I collaborate closely with stakeholders to understand their needs and objectives. I use techniques such as MoSCoW prioritization (Must have, Should have, Could have, Won't have) to categorize requirements based on their importance and urgency. I also consider factors such as business value, impact on project objectives, and feasibility to determine priorities. By engaging stakeholders in the prioritization process and aligning priorities with project goals, we can ensure that the most critical requirements are addressed first."

52. **Can you discuss your experience with conducting SWOT analysis to assess the strengths, weaknesses, opportunities, and threats of a project or organization?**
    - "I have experience conducting SWOT analysis to assess the internal and external factors that may impact a project or organization. I gather input from stakeholders and subject matter experts to identify strengths, weaknesses, opportunities, and threats across various areas such as market trends, competition, technology, and resources. I then analyze the findings to develop strategies that leverage strengths, address weaknesses, capitalize on opportunities, and mitigate threats. SWOT analysis provides valuable insights that inform decision-making and strategic planning, helping organizations maximize their competitive advantage and achieve their goals."

53. **How do you ensure that project deliverables meet quality standards and user expectations?**
    - "I ensure that project deliverables meet quality standards and user expectations by conducting thorough quality assurance activities throughout the project lifecycle. This includes reviewing requirements, design documents, and test plans to ensure alignment with stakeholder needs and objectives. I also conduct user acceptance testing (UAT) with representative end users to validate that deliverables meet their requirements and expectations. By incorporating feedback from stakeholders and users throughout the development process, we can identify and address issues

early, minimize rework, and deliver high-quality solutions that meet or exceed expectations."

54. **Can you provide an example of a time when you had to adapt to changes in project scope or requirements? How did you handle the situation?**
    - "In a previous project, there was a significant change in project scope due to shifting business priorities. To adapt to the changes, I conducted a thorough impact assessment to understand the implications on project objectives, timelines, and resources. I then collaborated with stakeholders to prioritize requirements and develop a revised project plan that aligned with the new scope. Throughout the process, I communicated transparently with stakeholders to manage expectations and ensure alignment with project goals. By remaining flexible and responsive to changing requirements, we were able to successfully navigate the changes and deliver value to the organization."

55. **How do you ensure effective communication and collaboration between technical and non-technical stakeholders?**
    - "I ensure effective communication and collaboration between technical and non-technical stakeholders by facilitating open dialogue, using clear and concise language, and leveraging visual aids or demonstrations to illustrate complex concepts. I also establish regular communication channels, such as meetings, status updates, and documentation reviews, to keep stakeholders informed and engaged throughout the project lifecycle. By fostering a collaborative environment where all stakeholders feel valued and heard, we can enhance understanding, build consensus, and drive successful outcomes."

56. **Can you discuss your experience with creating and managing project budgets as a business analyst?**
    - "I have experience creating and managing project budgets by collaborating with project sponsors, finance teams, and other stakeholders to define budgetary constraints and allocations. I work closely with project managers to develop

cost estimates, track expenses, and monitor budget variances throughout the project lifecycle. I also identify opportunities for cost savings or optimization and make recommendations to stakeholders to ensure that projects are delivered within budgetary constraints. By actively managing project budgets and resources, we can optimize project outcomes and maximize return on investment."

57. **How do you approach conducting stakeholder analysis and identifying key stakeholders for a project?**
    - "When conducting stakeholder analysis, I start by identifying all potential stakeholders and mapping out their roles, interests, and influence levels. I then prioritize stakeholders based on their level of impact on the project and their level of support or resistance. This helps me determine the most effective strategies for engaging with stakeholders and managing their expectations throughout the project lifecycle. By conducting thorough stakeholder analysis, we can build strong relationships, foster collaboration, and ensure stakeholder buy-in for project success."

58. **Can you discuss your experience with facilitating requirements gathering sessions and eliciting requirements from stakeholders?**
    - "I have extensive experience with facilitating requirements gathering sessions and eliciting requirements from stakeholders using techniques such as interviews, workshops, surveys, and observation. I create a collaborative environment that encourages open communication and active participation from all stakeholders. I also use visualization tools such as diagrams, prototypes, or mockups to help stakeholders visualize and articulate their requirements more effectively. By engaging stakeholders in the requirements gathering process, we can ensure that their needs are accurately captured and incorporated into the project solution."

59. **How do you ensure that project requirements are effectively communicated to technical teams for implementation?**

- "I ensure that project requirements are effectively communicated to technical teams for implementation by developing clear and concise documentation, such as functional specifications or user stories, that outline the requirements in detail. I also conduct regular meetings or workshops with technical teams to review requirements, clarify any ambiguities, and address questions or concerns. Additionally, I provide ongoing support and clarification throughout the development process to ensure that requirements are understood and implemented accurately. By maintaining open communication and collaboration between business and technical teams, we can minimize misunderstandings, reduce rework, and deliver solutions that meet stakeholder needs."

60. **How do you handle situations where stakeholders have conflicting or competing priorities?**
    - "When stakeholders have conflicting priorities, I facilitate open communication and collaboration to understand their underlying interests and concerns. I use techniques such as negotiation, consensus-building, and compromise to find common ground and reach mutually acceptable solutions. If necessary, I escalate conflicts to project sponsors or senior leadership for resolution, while ensuring transparency and accountability throughout the process. By fostering a collaborative approach to conflict resolution, we can build consensus, align priorities, and move projects forward effectively."

61. **How do you approach conducting gap analysis to identify discrepancies between current and desired states in a project?**
    - "I approach conducting gap analysis by first defining the current state and desired future state of the project. I then identify the gaps or discrepancies between the two states by comparing factors such as processes, systems, resources, and performance metrics. This helps me understand where improvements or changes are needed to bridge the gap and

achieve the desired outcomes. I collaborate closely with stakeholders to prioritize gap closure activities and develop actionable plans to address identified gaps."

62. **Can you discuss your experience with creating and maintaining project schedules or timelines?**
    - "I have experience creating and maintaining project schedules or timelines by developing detailed project plans that outline key tasks, milestones, and dependencies. I use project management software such as Microsoft Project or Trello to create Gantt charts or Kanban boards that visualize project timelines and progress. I also regularly monitor and update project schedules to track progress, identify potential delays or risks, and adjust timelines as needed to ensure project objectives are met."

63. **How do you ensure that project deliverables meet accessibility standards and accommodate diverse user needs?**
    - "I ensure that project deliverables meet accessibility standards and accommodate diverse user needs by incorporating accessibility considerations into the design and development process from the outset. I collaborate with accessibility experts, user experience designers, and subject matter experts to identify accessibility requirements and best practices. I also conduct usability testing with diverse user groups, including individuals with disabilities, to identify barriers and make necessary adjustments to ensure that project deliverables are inclusive and accessible to all users."

64. **Can you discuss your experience with conducting business process modeling and optimization?**
    - "I have experience conducting business process modeling and optimization by analyzing existing processes, identifying inefficiencies or bottlenecks, and designing improved or optimized processes. I use techniques such as process mapping, swimlane diagrams, and value stream mapping to visualize and analyze workflows. I also collaborate with stakeholders to identify opportunities for automation, standardization, or streamlining to improve efficiency, reduce costs, and enhance overall performance."

65. **How do you approach conducting post-project reviews or lessons learned sessions to identify areas for improvement?**
    - "I approach conducting post-project reviews or lessons learned sessions by gathering feedback from project stakeholders, including team members, sponsors, and customers, through surveys, interviews, or focus groups. I analyze the feedback to identify areas of success, challenges, and opportunities for improvement. I then facilitate discussions to discuss lessons learned, identify best practices, and develop actionable recommendations for future projects. By promoting a culture of continuous improvement, we can leverage insights from past experiences to drive better outcomes in future projects."
66. **Can you provide an example of a time when you had to lead a cross-functional team on a project?**
    - "In a previous project, I led a cross-functional team comprised of members from different departments, including IT, operations, and finance, to implement a new enterprise resource planning (ERP) system. I facilitated regular meetings and workshops to align team members on project objectives, roles, and responsibilities. I also established clear communication channels and protocols to facilitate collaboration and decision-making. Through effective leadership and teamwork, we successfully implemented the ERP system on time and within budget."
67. **How do you ensure that project communication plans are effective in keeping stakeholders informed and engaged throughout the project lifecycle?**
    - "I ensure that project communication plans are effective by developing clear communication objectives, channels, and protocols that align with project goals and stakeholder needs. I establish regular communication schedules and formats, such as status updates, meetings, or newsletters, to keep stakeholders informed of project progress, milestones, and key decisions. I also encourage two-way communication and feedback to foster engagement and collaboration among stakeholders."

68. **Can you discuss your experience with conducting user training and change management activities to support the adoption of new systems or processes?**
    - "I have experience conducting user training and change management activities by developing tailored training plans and materials that address the specific needs and preferences of end users. I use a combination of training methods, such as in-person workshops, online tutorials, and job aids, to accommodate different learning styles and preferences. I also incorporate change management principles and techniques, such as communication plans, stakeholder engagement, and readiness assessments, to prepare users for the transition and minimize resistance to change."

69. **How do you ensure that project requirements are traceable, testable, and verifiable throughout the project lifecycle?**
    - "I ensure that project requirements are traceable, testable, and verifiable by using techniques such as requirements traceability matrices (RTMs) and validation and verification processes. I establish clear links between requirements, design specifications, and test cases to ensure that each requirement is addressed and validated through testing. I also conduct regular reviews and inspections to verify that requirements are complete, consistent, and aligned with stakeholder needs and objectives."

70. **Can you discuss your experience with conducting risk management and how you identify, assess, and mitigate risks on projects?**
    - "I have experience with risk management by identifying, assessing, and mitigating risks on projects. I conduct risk assessments to identify potential threats or opportunities that may impact project objectives, timelines, or resources. I then develop risk mitigation strategies to minimize the likelihood and impact of risks, such as contingency plans, risk transfer, or risk avoidance strategies. Throughout the project

lifecycle, I regularly monitor risks and take proactive steps to address emerging threats or capitalize on opportunities."

71. **How do you ensure that project requirements are captured accurately and comprehensively from stakeholders with varying levels of domain knowledge?**
- "To ensure accurate and comprehensive requirement capture, I employ various elicitation techniques tailored to stakeholders' backgrounds, such as interviews, workshops, and document analysis. I use plain language and visual aids to facilitate understanding, and I validate requirements iteratively with stakeholders to ensure alignment. Additionally, I leverage subject matter experts to fill knowledge gaps and verify technical feasibility, ensuring that requirements are captured accurately across all levels of domain knowledge."

72. **Can you discuss your experience with conducting feasibility studies to assess the viability of proposed projects or solutions?**
- "I have conducted feasibility studies to assess the viability of projects or solutions by evaluating technical, economic, and operational factors. I gather data on costs, benefits, risks, and constraints to determine the feasibility of various options. I analyze the findings using techniques such as cost-benefit analysis, risk assessment, and SWOT analysis to make informed recommendations. By conducting thorough feasibility studies, I help stakeholders make strategic decisions and prioritize investments that align with organizational goals and objectives."

73. **How do you approach conducting root cause analysis to identify underlying factors contributing to project issues or challenges?**
- "I approach root cause analysis by employing techniques such as fishbone diagrams, 5 Whys, or Pareto analysis to systematically identify underlying factors contributing to project issues or challenges. I collaborate with stakeholders to gather data and insights, analyze patterns and trends, and identify potential root

causes. I then prioritize root causes based on their impact and feasibility of addressing them, and develop targeted solutions or corrective actions to address the underlying issues and prevent recurrence."

74. **Can you discuss your experience with facilitating workshops or focus groups to gather input and feedback from stakeholders?**
- "I have facilitated workshops or focus groups to gather input and feedback from stakeholders using structured facilitation techniques and activities. I design workshop agendas and exercises that encourage active participation, creativity, and collaboration among participants. I also use facilitation tools such as brainstorming, affinity diagramming, or SWOT analysis to generate ideas, prioritize options, and make decisions collaboratively. By creating a supportive and inclusive environment, I can effectively elicit valuable insights and perspectives from stakeholders."

75. **How do you ensure that project deliverables are aligned with regulatory or compliance requirements?**
- "I ensure that project deliverables are aligned with regulatory or compliance requirements by conducting thorough research and analysis to understand relevant laws, regulations, and industry standards. I work closely with legal and compliance teams to identify applicable requirements and ensure that project plans, requirements, and deliverables are designed to meet or exceed regulatory standards. I also conduct regular reviews and audits to verify compliance throughout the project lifecycle."

76. **Can you discuss your experience with creating and maintaining business process documentation, such as process maps, flowcharts, and standard operating procedures (SOPs)?**
- "I have experience creating and maintaining business process documentation by capturing processes using techniques such as process mapping, flowcharting, and swimlane diagrams. I collaborate with process owners and subject matter experts to document current state processes, identify opportunities for improvement, and design future state processes. I also develop standard operating procedures (SOPs) and process manuals to standardize workflows and ensure consistency in operations. By

documenting processes effectively, I help organizations streamline operations, improve efficiency, and maintain compliance."

77. **How do you facilitate requirements prioritization sessions with stakeholders to ensure alignment and consensus?**

- "I facilitate requirements prioritization sessions by engaging stakeholders in a structured process that encourages open communication and collaboration. I start by presenting a prioritization framework, such as MoSCoW (Must have, Should have, Could have, Won't have), and providing context on project objectives and constraints. I then guide stakeholders through the prioritization process, using techniques such as voting, ranking, or pairwise comparison to identify and prioritize requirements. Throughout the session, I foster discussion, manage conflicts, and facilitate consensus-building to ensure alignment and commitment to the prioritized requirements."

78. **How do you approach conducting user acceptance testing (UAT) to ensure that project deliverables meet user needs and expectations?**

- "I approach conducting user acceptance testing (UAT) by collaborating with end users to define acceptance criteria, develop test scenarios, and execute test cases. I ensure that UAT is conducted in a controlled environment that mirrors the production environment as closely as possible. I provide guidance and support to users throughout the testing process, addressing any questions or issues that arise. I also document and track defects, prioritize resolution based on severity and impact, and verify fixes to ensure that project deliverables meet user needs and expectations."

79. **Can you provide an example of a time when you had to manage project dependencies and mitigate risks to ensure project success?**

- "In a previous project, we faced challenges with managing project dependencies and mitigating risks due to delays in vendor deliveries and resource constraints. To address these issues, I conducted a thorough analysis of dependencies and risks, prioritizing critical path activities and developing contingency plans. I collaborated closely with vendors and stakeholders to expedite deliveries, reallocate resources, and adjust timelines as needed. By proactively managing dependencies and risks, we were able to mitigate potential impacts and ensure project success."

80. **How do you ensure effective communication and collaboration within project teams, especially in virtual or remote work environments?**
- "I ensure effective communication and collaboration within project teams by leveraging technology tools such as video conferencing, project management software, and collaboration platforms. I establish clear communication channels, expectations, and protocols to facilitate regular updates, progress reports, and feedback loops. I also foster a culture of transparency, trust, and accountability, where team members feel comfortable sharing ideas, asking questions, and addressing concerns. Additionally, I schedule regular team meetings and check-ins to maintain engagement and alignment, especially in virtual or remote work environments."

81. **How do you approach conducting stakeholder interviews to gather requirements and insights?**
- "I approach stakeholder interviews by preparing a structured agenda that covers key topics and objectives. I use active listening and probing techniques to encourage stakeholders to share their perspectives, needs, and expectations openly. I also ask open-ended questions to uncover insights and elicit detailed requirements. Throughout the interview, I take detailed notes and seek clarification on any ambiguous or unclear points. By conducting thorough stakeholder interviews, I ensure that requirements are accurately captured and aligned with stakeholder needs."

82. **Can you discuss your experience with documenting business requirements using various techniques such as use cases, user stories, and functional specifications?**
- "I have experience documenting business requirements using various techniques such as use cases, user stories, and functional specifications. I collaborate with stakeholders to define clear and concise requirements that capture user needs, system functionality,

and acceptance criteria. I use use cases to describe system interactions from the user's perspective, user stories to capture user requirements in a concise format, and functional specifications to detail system behavior and requirements in technical terms. By employing a variety of documentation techniques, I ensure that requirements are communicated effectively to both business and technical stakeholders."

83. **How do you handle situations where project scope or requirements change mid-project?**

- "When project scope or requirements change mid-project, I conduct a thorough impact analysis to assess the implications on project objectives, timelines, and resources. I communicate the changes transparently to stakeholders and collaborate with them to evaluate trade-offs and prioritize requirements. If necessary, I update project documentation, such as project plans, requirements documents, and schedules, to reflect the changes. By managing scope changes effectively and maintaining alignment with project goals, we can adapt to evolving requirements while minimizing disruptions to project delivery."

84. **Can you provide an example of a time when you successfully managed a project under tight deadlines and resource constraints?**

- "In a previous project, we faced tight deadlines and resource constraints due to unexpected changes in business requirements and staffing issues. To successfully manage the project under these constraints, I conducted a rapid assessment of project priorities, risks, and dependencies. I re-allocated resources and reprioritized tasks to focus on critical path activities and deliverables. I also negotiated with stakeholders to streamline approval processes and reduce unnecessary bureaucracy. Through proactive planning, effective communication, and resourceful problem-solving, we were able to meet the project deadlines and deliver value to the organization."

85. **How do you ensure that project deliverables are aligned with business objectives and provide measurable value to stakeholders?**

- "I ensure that project deliverables are aligned with business objectives by establishing clear success criteria and performance metrics that link project outcomes to organizational goals. I collaborate with stakeholders to define key performance indicators (KPIs) and acceptance criteria that measure the effectiveness and impact of project deliverables. Throughout the project lifecycle, I track and report on progress against these metrics, making adjustments as needed to ensure alignment with business objectives. By demonstrating measurable value to stakeholders, we can validate project success and drive continuous improvement."

86. **Can you discuss your experience with conducting data analysis to identify trends, patterns, and insights that inform business decisions?**

- "I have experience conducting data analysis to identify trends, patterns, and insights that inform business decisions. I gather data from various sources, such as databases, spreadsheets, and business intelligence tools, and use statistical and analytical techniques to analyze and interpret the data. I visualize the findings using charts, graphs, and dashboards to communicate insights effectively to stakeholders. I also conduct root cause analysis to understand underlying factors driving trends and patterns, and make data-driven recommendations to support informed decision-making."

87. **How do you approach facilitating requirements prioritization sessions with stakeholders to ensure alignment and consensus?**

- "I approach requirements prioritization sessions by engaging stakeholders in a structured process that encourages open communication and collaboration. I start by presenting a prioritization framework, such as MoSCoW (Must have, Should have, Could have, Won't have), and providing context on project objectives and constraints. I then guide stakeholders through the prioritization process, using techniques such as voting, ranking, or pairwise comparison to identify and prioritize requirements. Throughout the session, I foster discussion, manage conflicts, and facilitate consensus-building to ensure alignment and commitment to the prioritized requirements."

88. **How do you ensure that project requirements are validated and verified to meet stakeholder needs and expectations?**
- "I ensure that project requirements are validated and verified by conducting thorough reviews, inspections, and testing throughout the project lifecycle. I engage stakeholders in user acceptance testing (UAT) to validate that requirements meet their needs and expectations. I also conduct peer reviews and inspections to verify that requirements are complete, consistent, and aligned with project objectives. Additionally, I use traceability matrices and validation processes to ensure that each requirement is addressed and verified through testing. By validating and verifying requirements effectively, we can minimize rework and deliver solutions that meet stakeholder needs."

89. **How do you approach conducting risk identification and analysis to proactively mitigate project risks?**
- "I approach risk identification and analysis by engaging stakeholders in a structured process that systematically identifies and evaluates potential risks to project objectives, timelines, and resources. I use techniques such as brainstorming, SWOT analysis, and risk registers to capture and prioritize risks based on their likelihood and impact. I collaborate with stakeholders to develop risk mitigation strategies that reduce the likelihood and impact of identified risks. I also monitor and track risks throughout the project lifecycle, making adjustments as needed to ensure proactive risk management."

90. **Can you provide an example of a time when you had to communicate complex technical concepts or requirements to non-technical stakeholders?**
- "In a previous project, I had to communicate complex technical concepts related to a new software implementation to non-technical stakeholders, such as business users and senior leadership. To do this effectively, I used plain language and analogies to simplify complex concepts and make them more accessible. I also used visual aids such as diagrams, charts, and prototypes to illustrate key concepts and facilitate understanding. Additionally, I encouraged two-way communication and welcomed

questions and feedback to ensure that stakeholders felt comfortable and engaged throughout the communication process."

91. **How do you approach conducting stakeholder analysis and managing stakeholder expectations throughout the project lifecycle?**

- "I approach stakeholder analysis by identifying key stakeholders, understanding their interests, influence, and expectations, and developing tailored communication and engagement plans to address their needs. I regularly communicate with stakeholders, provide updates on project progress, and solicit feedback to ensure alignment and manage expectations. By building strong relationships and fostering open communication, I can effectively engage stakeholders and secure their support throughout the project lifecycle."

92. **Can you discuss your experience with creating business requirements documents (BRDs) and functional requirements documents (FRDs)?**

- "I have experience creating business requirements documents (BRDs) and functional requirements documents (FRDs) by collaborating with stakeholders to capture business needs, objectives, and functional specifications. I use techniques such as interviews, workshops, and document analysis to elicit and document requirements in a clear, concise, and structured manner. I also ensure that requirements are traceable, testable, and aligned with project goals and objectives. By developing comprehensive BRDs and FRDs, I provide a solid foundation for project planning, design, and development."

93. **How do you approach conducting user research and gathering user feedback to inform project decisions and enhancements?**

- "I approach conducting user research by employing techniques such as surveys, interviews, focus groups, and usability testing to gather insights and feedback from end users. I collaborate with user experience designers and usability experts to design research studies and develop test scenarios that address key research objectives. I analyze the findings to identify user needs, pain points, and preferences, and make data-driven recommendations to inform project decisions and enhancements. By incorporating user feedback throughout the design and development process, we can create solutions that are intuitive, user-friendly, and aligned with user needs."

94. **Can you provide an example of a time when you had to manage scope creep on a project? How did you address it?**
- "In a previous project, we encountered scope creep due to changing business requirements and stakeholder requests. To address it, I conducted a thorough impact assessment to understand the implications on project objectives, timelines, and resources. I collaborated with stakeholders to prioritize requirements and manage expectations. I also implemented change control processes to document and evaluate scope changes, assess their impact on project constraints, and obtain approval from project sponsors before implementing them. By managing scope creep proactively, we were able to minimize its impact on project success."

95. **How do you ensure that project deliverables are aligned with strategic business objectives and priorities?**
- "I ensure that project deliverables are aligned with strategic business objectives and priorities by collaborating closely with stakeholders to understand their strategic goals and objectives. I conduct thorough analysis and assessment to ensure that project initiatives are directly linked to strategic priorities and contribute to overall business value. I also develop key performance indicators (KPIs) and metrics to measure the impact and effectiveness of project deliverables in achieving strategic objectives. By aligning project activities and outcomes with strategic priorities, we can maximize the value and impact of our projects."

96. **Can you discuss your experience with conducting business process reengineering (BPR) and driving organizational change?**
- "I have experience conducting business process reengineering (BPR) by analyzing existing processes, identifying opportunities for improvement, and redesigning processes to achieve organizational goals and objectives. I collaborate with stakeholders to define

desired outcomes, assess current state processes, and develop future state process models that streamline workflows, eliminate inefficiencies, and enhance performance. I also develop change management strategies and communication plans to facilitate adoption and implementation of new processes, ensuring that organizational change is managed effectively and stakeholders are engaged throughout the process."

97. **How do you approach conducting cost-benefit analysis to evaluate the financial implications of proposed projects or solutions?**

- "I approach conducting cost-benefit analysis by quantifying the costs and benefits associated with proposed projects or solutions and comparing them to determine their financial viability and return on investment (ROI). I gather data on costs such as capital expenditures, operating expenses, and resource allocation, and estimate potential benefits such as increased revenue, cost savings, and productivity gains. I also consider intangible benefits such as improved customer satisfaction or competitive advantage. By conducting thorough cost-benefit analysis, I provide stakeholders with objective data and insights to make informed decisions about resource allocation and investment."

98. **Can you discuss your experience with developing business cases to justify investments in projects or initiatives?**

- "I have experience developing business cases to justify investments in projects or initiatives by analyzing the strategic alignment, financial feasibility, and potential benefits of proposed initiatives. I conduct market research, competitive analysis, and risk assessments to assess the business opportunity and identify key success factors. I also develop financial models, such as net present value (NPV), return on investment (ROI), and payback period, to quantify the financial impact and justify the investment. By developing compelling business cases, I help stakeholders make informed decisions and secure funding for strategic initiatives."

99. **How do you ensure that project requirements are effectively communicated and understood by technical and non-technical stakeholders?**

- "I ensure that project requirements are effectively communicated and understood by technical and non-technical stakeholders by using clear and concise language, visual aids, and demonstrations to illustrate concepts and requirements. I tailor communication methods and formats to the preferences and needs of different stakeholders, such as using diagrams, prototypes, or mockups for technical stakeholders, and plain language summaries or presentations for non-technical stakeholders. I also facilitate discussions, workshops, and reviews to solicit feedback, clarify ambiguities, and ensure that requirements are accurately understood and interpreted by all stakeholders."

100. **Can you provide an example of a time when you had to lead a cross-functional team to deliver a complex project? How did you ensure collaboration and alignment across different departments?**

- "In a previous project, I led a cross-functional team comprised of members from different departments, including IT, operations, and marketing, to implement a new customer relationship management (CRM) system. To ensure collaboration and alignment across departments, I established clear project objectives, roles, and responsibilities, and fostered a culture of teamwork and accountability. I facilitated regular meetings and workshops to align team members on project goals, priorities, and milestones. I also established clear communication channels and protocols to facilitate collaboration, address issues, and make decisions collaboratively. By promoting open communication and collaboration, we were able to successfully deliver the project on time and within budget, meeting the needs of all stakeholders."

www.ingramcontent.com/pod-product-compliance
Lightning Source LLC
Chambersburg PA
CBHW062235220526
45471CB00009B/3496